Good Grief

When Grief Meets Grace

SAMARA BRENNAN

WESTBOW
PRESS

A DIVISION OF THOMAS NELSON

WestBow Press books may be ordered through booksellers or by contacting:

WestBow Press
A Division of Thomas Nelson
1663 Liberty Drive
Bloomington, IN 47403
www.westbowpress.com
1-(866) 928-1240

ISBN: 978-1-4497-9119-3 (sc)
ISBN: 978-1-4497-9121-6 (hc)
ISBN: 978-1-4497-9120-9 (e)

Library of Congress Control Number: 2013906389

Printed in the United States of America.

WestBow Press rev. date: 4/12/2013

Table of Contents

—⁓∘◦◦◦⦿◦◦⁓—

Dedication

Nathan Dean Brennan,
born in glory
August 8, 2011

And to
my Savior,
who makes it all possible.
Thank you for giving me hope
and a future.

Acknowledgments

———～ⅿ•๑๑✵✵✵✵๑๑•ⅿ～———

To James, thank you for believing when I could not. Thank you for your unwavering support and faithfulness. Thank you for sharing this journey with me and for the laughter through the tears.

To Arlene, thank you for becoming my daughter. Thank you for making me a mama and for the cuddles. You will always be my child and be a sweet song in my heart.

To our family, thank you for your fervent prayers. Your dedication to our healing has been a beacon of hope and strength. Your support means everything. Thank you for believing in us.

To our friends, we praise God every day for you. Thank you for becoming our family and loving Nathan as your own.

Foreword

Everyone has met disappointment, heartache, and devastation at some point in life. No greater pain came to our family than the hurt that came on August 8, 2011. There, we were gathered in one room and said good-bye to a dream, a hope, an answered prayer—my nephew Nathan. We never got to hear his laugh or his cry, but we desperately missed him. Missed him? Some may say, "But you never knew him." No, we never had the privilege of getting to know Nathan, but we grieved over the loss of expectation, the loss of future hugs, kisses, and joy.

Some of you reading this book may not have directly experienced the sting of a child dying. Some of you may be reading this book to understand how to help someone you love cope with the death of a child. But all of you reading this book have at some point (or you will in the future) experienced loss in some sense of the word, and you will begin to realize that God doesn't work in the scope of our understanding.

Through Samara's journey, which is not yet fulfilled, you will have the chance to see a raw, bleeding faith in the face of doubt. Hopefully, you will conclude with a deeper sense that though dreams may not come to fruition and expectations often disappoint, God is still "I AM." So with tears, groaning, curses, and questions, come those who are weary, lonely, childless, empty-handed, and heavyhearted, come … and God will give you rest.

—Crystal Johnson

Preface

—⁓⦵⧟⦵⧟⁓—

I was not sure what to do with the crushing weight and ache of losing Nathan. I suffered years of infertility. And then without any help from modern medicine, we suddenly had a miracle! A baby! We felt joy, unspeakable joy! For the next nine months, I had a perfect pregnancy. And then he was gone. In a blink of an eye, he was gone without any earthly explanation.

It was suggested that I write letters to Nathan. However, the emotion was so raw that I could only write a few words before I crumbled into sadness. I wanted desperately to connect with him, to have some tangible reminder of his existence. I decided to try writing about him instead of writing to him, and suddenly, the healing began. After just a few entries, it was Christmastime. I was able to write to Nathan. I was able to tell him how much I adored him and connect with him despite his absence. Through the Lord, this was suddenly possible.

Sometime after I began writing about Nathan, I remembered that I had received a book shortly after his death. The title was very sad, and it was a bit thick. I imagine it ministered to many people, but it just wasn't what I was looking for. I thought, *There needs to be a small book of inspiration.* I thought that there needed to be a book that did not just focus on the desperation of infant loss but also pointed to the peace and grace I was experiencing. And so this book began.

I spent sleepless nights with my grief, allowing myself to feel it all, and poured it all out into the words you will find within these pages. I found that even through the tears, I was not helpless. These words brought me closer to Nathan. These words brought me to the other side of something unimaginable. The Lord met me each sleepless night and revealed himself in every entry.

I share this with you in the hopes that you, too, will be brought to the other side of such pain. I hope that the Holy Spirit leads you to peace even in your anguish. I share your sorrow. I share in your search for the answers that we may never find this side of heaven. I share Nathan with you, hoping you will realize you are not alone.

Children who are born in God's glory have a purpose beyond our understanding. For those of us left without them, the ache is real. The questions are often unanswered. The uncertainty is overwhelming. However, in all of this, the Lord is present. He does not leave us here alone. God's love is real, and He finds us in the broken places. He gives us peace beyond any understanding. Within these pages, I hope to share this abundant peace with you. We are on this journey together.

Chapter 1

What in the World Happened?

On Sunday, August 7, 2011, nine months into a miracle pregnancy, my husband and I bounced upstairs to the maternity floor in anticipation of our induction. We were preparing to meet our baby boy, Nathan, the very next morning. We took out our belongings and began to prepare our delivery room with the little odds and ends we had brought from home.

I was told to fill out a few forms and to put on the "designer" robe handed to me. My husband made himself at home on the bench, which would serve as his bed in a few short hours. He took out his laptop while the nurse helped me get up on the bed for a standard check of baby Nathan's vitals. I was all hooked up and looking good, but for some reason, she had a hard time finding baby boy's heartbeat.

James heard this and slowly closed his laptop. He set it on his bed. He slowly walked across the room, stood next to me, and held my hand. We were both very quiet, but James asked, "Is there a problem with the heartbeat?" We were told that she was just going to go get another monitor because sometimes they gave out and that she would be right back.

The nurse was gone for only a few minutes. During this time, James found the stool next to me and held my hand. We didn't say a word, and I didn't know if he could see the tears that had already started to trickle down my cheeks. I didn't know if he knew that I could see all the color draining from his face. And then our nurse was back with a new monitor and a new nurse in tow. The confusion began. "When is the last time you felt baby move? Have you been having problems with high blood pressure?" Then the nurse shook my belly slightly while she again asked, "When is the last time you felt the baby move?"

A sort of fog began to settle over me, and I don't remember speaking or seeing where James was in the room. My nurse touched my right hand softly, said they were going to get a sonogram technician, and left the room. It was just James and me. James pulled up the stool, held my hands, and kissed my cheek over and over. I closed my eyes and softly wept because I already knew.

The sonogram technician hooked me up, and the room was eerily quiet. No one said a word, but they didn't have to. As I lay silently weeping, all hospital personnel quietly exited our room. My original nurse came in, sat next to me, slowly caressed my hand, and said, "Sweetheart, I am so sorry." At that very moment, we said hello and good-bye to Nathan. *Shalom,* sweet angel. Only twenty-five minutes after we had arrived expecting a baby, we had to come to terms with leaving in a few days without him. We had arrived with a car seat ready to take him home, and in the blink of an eye, we had to accept that we would be leaving without him.

Shalom[1]

Shalom, little one, shalom. Hello. Good-bye.
Peace be with you.
With our time so short,
we had to find one word to say it all. Shalom.
We rejoiced in anticipation of greeting you. Hello.
And we grieve that you could not remain with us. Good-bye.
We marveled at your budding life within me and shall carry
you in our hearts with love.
Hello, my little one, and good-bye. Peace be with you. Shalom.

---

[1] Poem "Shalom," author unknown.

Chapter 2

Peace and Prayer

From the moment we learned Nathan had left us, I felt God's presence roll over me like a fog from the top of my head to the bottom of my feet. I felt only what I can describe as a peace blanket.

I will never forget how God revealed Himself to me that night. This was my "burning bush" moment—a moment when I could not deny Him. It was a supernatural experience that I still cherish today. As painful as not having Nathan is—hear me out on this—I would not trade him being here for God revealing Himself to me. Don't misunderstand me. I want my son here. I ache for his chubby fingers to wrap around mine. Luckily, I did not have to choose between Nathan being here now and my Creator showing me His real presence. I am lucky that God made this choice for me.

God revealed Himself to me despite my cries to take my life instead. God revealed Himself to me, even though I honestly hoped I would perish in delivery. I couldn't imagine living without Nathan. Yet God revealed Himself to me—stubborn, broken, full of yuck … me.

Chris Tomlin and Audrey Assad sing a song called "Winter Snow."[2] This song describes how Jesus could have come to us any way He wanted. He could have come to us in a grand display, but He came more softly. As the song says, "You could've come like a mighty storm, with all of the strength of a hurricane. You could've come like a forest fire, with the power of heaven in your flame. But you came like a winter snow, quiet, soft, and slow, falling from the sky in the night to the earth below."

I heard this song shortly after Nathan's death, and it brought me to tears. I relate to it differently than the way the writers probably intended; however, this is how I felt that night. God could have saved Nathan's life. Even the next morning, as Nathan was delivered, God could have breathed life into Nathan. He could have shown His power in a grand display, but instead, He came to us quietly—like a fog—and covered me in a peace blanket.

I don't pray to a God that I created. I pray to a God that created me. He is not sitting around, waiting on my instruction. He is not going to do what I want, but He is always going to answer. For years, my mom has said, "God has three answers: *yes, no,* and *wait.*"

That night, God said *no* when I begged. He said *no* when my sister was facedown on the floor, begging. He said *no* to my husband, who begged at my bedside. But He said *yes* to the countless others praying for our comfort.

---

[2] "Winter Snow," (featuring Audrey Assad) Chris Tomlin, *Glory in the Highest*, 2009.

I don't pray because it necessarily changes the outcome. I pray because it changes me. It changes how I see things. It allows me a glimpse of God and how He sees things. I pray because it unleashes the power of God in my heart. Prayer does not mean I get what I choose. God is going to do what is in His will to do—what He has had planned from the beginning of creation. Prayer does not change God, but it does change things.

Prayer will not bring Nathan back from the grave. It does, however, take away the darkness of his grave. Prayer is often bittersweet but still good medicine.

Chapter 3

Say What You Need to Say

Four months after Nathan passed away, I stopped to think about time. That takes a minute to sink in, doesn't it? Four months already? Four months, sixteen weeks, 121.74 days, 2,921.93 hours. But who's counting, right? It really does feel like yesterday sometimes, but other times, it feels a bit farther away. It is an awkward balance of time. It is hard not to count each minute of the day. It is a strange way of gauging how far you have made it each day, as if to say, "Well, I made it to noon. Let's see if I can make it to four o'clock!"

I have read that there are five stages of grief: denial, anger, bargaining, depression, and acceptance. The thing you don't read is that these stages do not always come in that order. Sometimes you can bounce back and forth between them in one day. I have found that in moving forward, it cannot be all about Nathan all the time. This was excruciating to accept but necessary for my mental health. How do I move forward without feeling as if I have left him behind?

It is necessary to move forward, even though you will never really move on. You have to find ways to accept the person you are becoming now and not look back to who you were. You have to accept that things are different but that different doesn't have to be horrible. You have to carry your loss with you but not let it smother you, letting your hope endure, so to speak. You have to find new joy, even if you have to try several times a day. So how do I find some semblance of normality and not make everything about losing Nathan?

I chose to start a blog. It became a place where it could be all about him during designated times. I could go there and write about my feelings as much as I wanted without worrying if talking about him would be painful or joyful. I didn't have to worry about bursting into tears or my knees buckling at the sound of his name.

Journaling in any format allows me to take my time and sit with any emotion—even ramble if I want to—because that is what this grief is like. But when I am done, I can make peace with it and walk away, having purged my emotion without letting it build into a grief monster.

At the end of the day, this was God's will. I have accepted that fact, even though I don't understand it. I have accepted that there will never be an answer to why. I will live my whole life and never know why God took Nathan. This side of heaven, there will not be answers, but one day, I will be reunited with him. When I finally get to hold Nathan again, this pain will no longer matter because we will both be in glory together.

I did not have a say in this. I am a work in progress, but above all, I have peace with you God.

Dear Lord,

I do not understand You, but I trust You. Thank You for accepting me unconditionally, even though I have to accept daily what You are doing in my life. I am sorry for yelling at You the other day ... Thank You for not yelling back :)

Why[3]

Why? That's what we ask. The truth is, we may never be able to know for sure why. But we do know that there is no single "should have done" or "could have done" or "did" or "didn't do" that would have changed that why. All that love could do was done

---

[3] Poem "Why," author unknown.

Chapter 4

Christmas

———∿∿∘⌒⊙⊙⌒∘⊙⌒∿∿———

Christmastime is often the "most wonderful time of the year." It should be, shouldn't it? It is the time when we celebrate Jesus' birth. It is when we celebrate that He came to us, all the while knowing that He would die for us. What a pure love Jesus has for us—to come here, to walk in our proverbial shoes, to feel our humanness, never sinning but knowing our struggle with sin.

Oh, how I miss Nathan. I was so looking forward to his first Christmas. I was so excited to tell him about baby Jesus. I wanted to see that twinkle in his eyes.

> *Nathan,*
>
> *You are so lucky to get to hang out with the Lord. I wonder every day what you are doing with Him. I wonder how it feels for you. I wonder what the word is to describe what Jesus' presence is like for you. I wonder if your chubby little fingers fit perfectly in Jesus' hands?*
>
> *Do you know how special you are? You have belonged to God from the very first moment. Maybe that is why you are with Him now. It is hard for Mommy*

to know that because you were God's to give, you were His to take.

When I am sad, I am not sad for you. I am only sad because I love you so very much and want to hug you and kiss you again. But I am reminded that you get plenty of hugs and kisses where you are. So today, I will try not to be so sad. I will do that for you, and one day, there will be no more tears for Mommy. Jesus will hug and kiss me too. And I will know the answers to all those questions. I will get to hold your chubby hands again. They were the most beautiful hands I've ever seen.

Love, Mommy

Lord,

I am waiting here for You. I know that in the stillness of my grief, You are there. Help me to know peace beyond understanding. Thank You for coming to me where I am and not making me search for You. Thank You for Your birth and for walking my walk before me. Help me with my steps. Actually, strike that. Please be my feet instead.

Chapter 5

Mercies in Disguise

Christmas came and went. I anticipated the pain of the first Christmas. It was like the smell of rain in the breeze right before a storm. My family and I planned a quiet Christmas, knowing how difficult the first without Nathan would be. Everyone in attendance was very encouraging and sensitive to our feelings. There were two little ones there, and it was bittersweet watching them both tear at the wrapping paper on their presents. It was sweet because I adored them both. Their sweet little faces brought smiles and laughter to the room. It was bitter because I couldn't help but think to myself that there should have been one more little one. Nathan should've been there too. There were moments when it hurt horribly, but then one of the other little ones would giggle or smile up at me. Somehow, that sweetness wrapped around me and made it all okay.

I expected the pain. Prepared for it the best I could. I guarded against the darkness with prayer, and I kind of sat and waited for the grief to knock me over. But a funny thing happened. I felt the grief. I was aware of it. I shed many tears, but it did not knock me over.

Grief is such a strange beast. I am not sure what is worse—the moments when missing Nathan hits me suddenly all at once taking my breath away or how it becomes almost an extension of my consciousness. I know it is there, but somehow, I was used to it. It is sort of like a dull headache that lingers behind your eyes all day, but you still manage.

Which is worse—not knowing when the pain is coming or accepting when it lingers? Is accepting it part of moving forward, or will that hold me back? Can you live with such a loss and truly live?

Laura Story sings a song called "Blessings." She sings, "Pain reminds this heart that this is not our home."[4] This aching is only temporary. It may never end this side of heaven, but for me, it will end someday. Perhaps the pain of missing Nathan is a mercy in disguise. Perhaps it is such a part of something so much bigger. Perhaps this trial is meant to reveal God. God has always been faithful to me, so why do I struggle with Him allowing Nathan's death for His purpose—a purpose that might be something glorious.

If I believe Nathan was a gift from God—that even being the literal meaning of his name—then I have to also believe that if He was God's, then he was God's to take. That being a hard pill to swallow does not make it untrue. If I am to believe what I believe, then I have to believe it all—the good, the bad, and the tragic. I have to accept it all and know that it is all temporary. It will not last forever, but Nathan will. In Christ, Nathan lives, and because I believe, so will I. That holds me. That keeps me. That is truth.

---

[4] "Blessings," Laura Story, *Blessings,* 2011.

Chapter 6

A Grief Observed

————〜〜•◦◦◦◦◦•〜〜————

I wish I could take credit for the title of this chapter. However, it comes from C.S. Lewis's work *A Grief Observed*.[5] I highly recommend this book with a small disclaimer.

First, he writes in his unique theologian manner. I had to look up a few words in the dictionary myself. So don't feel bad if you have to read a few sentences over again like I did.

Second, it is a very powerful book. He writes openly. He writes those things we think but never say out loud, the true feelings we somehow think we can hide from our Creator. It is powerful, reading Lewis's anger, questions, and uncertainty by relating to them in such a raw way. It is even more powerful, coming to terms with the acceptance he finds in the end. He bounces back and forth between the stages of grief, and he helped me to feel normal for also feeling this way. It helped guide me to a different place.

Not to say that I am okay with such a loss as Nathan. Not to say I do not have my moments of anger. And certainly not to

---

[5]   C. S. Lewis, *A Grief Observed* (Toronto: Bantam Books, 1961).

say that in my anguish I have not screamed to heaven, desperate for God to send Nathan back to us. But I will say that this book brought about things I was not even aware that I needed to come to terms with, namely feelings I am holding onto because I think they bring me closer to Nathan. When in reality, they only make him seem further away.

Who told me that the harder I cry, the better mother I am? Who told me that there is shame in me getting better? Who told me that there is shame in laughing? God never told me such things. The Enemy told me these things, of course.

He deceives me by leading me to believe that by moving forward, I love Nathan less. His lies lead me to think that without my baby here, I am no longer a mother. He shames me into thinking that my body is tainted and useless, that it led to Nathan's death somehow. He attacks me daily in the hope that I will turn and attack myself. But I think he underestimates *my God.*

I am not strong enough. I am desperate. I am weak. I am scared. But I am also tapped into the power of the one true *God.* Nothing can separate me from Him. So Mr. Enemy, you should realize you are wasting your time. You may knock me down— maybe even several times—but I am going to keep getting back up. I am not going to curse God or quit believing in His plan for my life. You are not going to make me turn my back on my Creator. I will doubt myself that is true, but my God will show me the truth. My God never lies. My God never leaves me. I will be sad, but my God will embrace me.

Simply put, I am learning that the harder I fight the Enemy and the less I mourn Nathan, the closer He is to me. I am Nathan's mother no matter where he is. He was born in glory, but that does not take away that he lived for nine months within me. My son is with God, and yet he is still my son.

> "The aching may remain, but the breaking does not."[6]

> —Andrew Peterson

Dear Lord,

Thank You for truth. It holds it all together, mainly me.

---

[6] "The Silence of God," Andrew Peterson, *Love and Thunder,* 2000.

Chapter 7

What Is Normal Anyway?

—⁓•◦⊙⧁⊙✦⊙◦•⁓—

Some days are not horrible. Sometimes I will be doing a simple chore like vacuuming, and I will have to sit down and cry for a bit. But then I am able to carry on, which makes for a pretty good day for me.

But these days are not without the realization. Nathan's absence will still hit me all at once. Most of the time, I carry missing him like a horrible headache. It is something I carry all day. I am aware of it, but I am able to function.

One day while I was vacuuming, for a split second, I wondered if the vacuum would wake Nathan up. Isn't that a wild thought? I know he is not here, but it is like my mind forgot for a moment and regarded him as present. As if he was just in another room. The rude awakening of reality snapped my knees a little, and I immediately corrected my thoughts. I thought, *I wonder if the vacuum* would have *woken Nathan up* if *he* was *here*.

It is strange. Sometimes it is like a dream, like this didn't really happen, But alas, it is true, and I know I am not crazy for these moments when my mind plays with what my heart knows is missing.

These moments actually make me feel as normal as possible. It is quite normal for a mother to think of her child. It is quite normal for me to regard Nathan and wonder about what he would be doing or how things would affect him. And even those split seconds of confusion are normal too.

The fact that I can bounce back from these moments is proof of my progress.

I am not even sure what normal is anyway. You can't put this loss in a box … or any other loss for that matter. What works for me may not work for someone else and vice versa. My grief is not the same as anyone else's, even if the situations are the same. The only thing I know for sure about grief is that it does not discriminate. It hits anyone at any time. It does not care who you are or what you have done. Good or bad, no one person stands out.

Those of us on the road of loss can only give each other landmarks as guides because our maps are all different. They have to be because our destinations are not the same. Up or down? Left or right? It is all confusion really, and in the end, the fact that none of us know the way alone helps me feel more normal. There isn't a shortcut I am missing. Others feel the way I do.

And while confusion exists … at least we are not alone, and if we *believe*, I think we will find that Jesus provides excellent maps and even shelter on the road. He was a carpenter after all.

Chapter 8

It's Okay

This morning was a difficult morning, *but that is okay.* This morning, I missed Nathan more than I can describe, *but that is okay.* This morning, I questioned God's plan for me, *but that is okay.* This morning, I felt a bit more restless, *but that is okay.* This morning, Satan taunted me with self-doubt about Nathan's death, making me feel guilt and filling my head with lies. *That is not okay.*

So I got out of bed, and in that one gesture, *I fought back.* I took a shower, and in that one gesture, *I fought back.* I got dressed and did not crawl back into bed. In that one gesture, *I fought back.*

Then I prayed, and in that one gesture, Satan fled. God wins every time. And that is more than okay.

Chapter 9

Open Communication

Some days, we have good "Nathan days." James and I use that type of blanket phrase because we must have constant communication between us about Nathan. Any moment can be good or bad, and it can be different for each of us at different times. If one of us is having a good "Nathan day," we have to be sensitive if the other isn't and vice versa. Resentment builds otherwise, and who needs that? It is important that when one of us is off, the other needs to be on. We have to be each other's soldiers. The loss of Nathan is the struggle of our collective lives thus far. Because of our open communication about Nathan, our marriage has never wavered. Our marriage is strong and solid. Keeping our focus on strengthening each other is how we can fight the Enemy. Satan wants Nathan's death to tear us apart. He wants the worst possible situation for us. That is why he is referred to as the Enemy.

The day of Nathan's funeral, we sat amongst our parents and asked for prayer over our marriage. I asked that they pray a blanket of protection that we not lose each other in all of this pain. I can say that this prayer of protection is still in full effect. This is a prayer in action.

We have found a way to talk to others about Nathan and walk away with what we now call a "Nathan glow." If I am in a situation and I start telling others about our loss, I normally and instantly feel James beside me. I don't always know how long he has been there. All I know is that he is there and that gives me strength. It brings me to an understanding of a statement James often makes. He says, "I love talking about Nathan with people. It never makes me sad. I am proud of my son." Seeing the pride James has in being Nathan's daddy allows me to hear above the noise in my mind and in my heart, and I can hear the Holy Spirit say, "Go ahead and talk about your boy."

We couldn't have come to this place of communication without a lot of late-night discussions. Discussions that are honest and safe can sustain a marriage through even your worst nightmare.

Chapter 10

Well Said, Paul

———〜〜∘ᕕᕗᕗᕗ∘〜〜———

Not that I have already obtained it or have
already become perfect, but I press on so that I
may lay hold of that which also I was laid hold
of by Christ Jesus. Brethren, I do not regard
myself as having laid hold of it yet; but one thing
I do: forgetting what lies behind and reaching
forward to what lies ahead, I press on toward the
goal for the prize of the upward call of God in
Christ Jesus.

—Philippians 3:12-14

Now, this is some good stuff. This is just one thing I love
about the Bible. It says exactly what I need to hear, exactly when
I need to hear it. I love how Paul speaks of pressing on, running
the race, so to speak. Not that we forget our little ones, but rather
we supplant the pain associated with losing them.

I will never forget Nathan. Nor should I. He remains a miracle
I am blessed to have experienced. I do not have to forget him, to
forget the aching and breaking of my heart. I can set him aside

from that pain and see him as a living gift from God. He just lives elsewhere in his glorified body and gets to hang out with Jesus every moment. What a lucky little booger.

The most amazing thing I have experienced this side of heaven was feeling Nathan grow within me. To feel his life is something I cherish. To see my belly grow as he grew was an awesome display. I loved every moment of expecting him. Now I must love every moment in anticipation of our reunion.

One day, I will stand before the Lord. One day, I will answer for my life. And even though I have questioned this trial and screamed of its unfairness, He will give me the gift of being reunited with Nathan. Seeing Jesus and praising Him in glory is the goal and will be the ultimate experience of my whole life. But He loves me so much that He will still give me Nathan. Now that is love. Even when it is all about Him, He will still consider me. Heaven is not about me and Nathan. But Jesus loves me to the point that He will still give that to me. He loves me that much.

Chapter 11

Progress

Six months passed, and I found it unbelievable. Sometimes it seems like yesterday. I would not say it has gotten any easier, but as time passes, I am more and more at peace. James and I now have a code word that we can whisper to each other if we are in a social situation and get sad enough to need to leave.

I read this idea in a book that one of my sister's professors sent us. It was mentioned by Professor Ballard.[7] He and his wife gave a name to this grief phenomenon. If they were in a public place or social setting and missing their son became too overwhelming, they would whisper their own code word, and the other would know they were hurting. It is a way to kindly wrap things up and just be with each other. I think it is a wonderful tool.

Six months into our grief journey, I found that taking expectation out of things allows me to be more flexible and be very at peace with not being in control. James and I know that Nathan lived the days he was meant to, and we did not fail him

---

[7] H. Wayne Ballard, Jr., PhD, associate professor, school of religion at Carson-Newman College, *Assaulted by Grief: Finding God in the Broken Places* (Mossy Creek Press, 2011), 63.

in any way. What is meant to happen will happen. God is in control, and I just have to surrender that He knows what is best for us. All I can do is hope and keep going forward. God knows the desires of my heart. He knows how much we wanted Nathan, and He knows how hard losing him has been for us. I am in the best hands, even if I don't understand.

Something that has been difficult is learning how to adjust to being in public or participating in anything social. I have always been slightly anxious in social situations, and I never really liked crowds. Now it has amplified.

I feel like I have a huge sign on me that screams, "Warning! Grieving mother who could cry at any time." Let's be honest. Ninety-nine percent of people are too busy with their own tasks to even notice me. And even if they do, they are certainly not even aware of my grief. So I know it is crazy talk, but still, it is a struggle. A breakdown in public has never even happened, but the fear of it can be debilitating.

One of the things I decided to do to overcome this debilitating fear and anxiety was to volunteer a few hours a week at a place I love. I choose the library because it fit my personality, but there are amazing opportunities out there for each and every one of us.

I met with the coordinator. And in a short time, I was volunteering a few hours per week, but it was a huge step. It helped move me back into social settings, and it forced me to overcome this crud.

I had to find something that was set apart from losing Nathan. I needed something that was just for me. I have to learn to separate myself from losing Nathan. Not everything can be about that.

I can choose certain outlets for that, like my blog, for example. There, it can be all about him all the time. It is a safe place. But I can't only focus on him. I have to live this life. Even if he had lived, it couldn't be all about him.

While I was making small talk shortly after I began volunteering, the conversation led someone to ask if I had any children. I, of course, told him about my much older, adopted daughter Arlene and followed it up with how James and I hoped to add to that one day. It felt like the situation was running in slow motion. I did not mention Nathan, even though I was thinking about him. But for the first time, I felt okay with not mentioning him. I did not feel guilty about not opening up the wound. I felt okay with thinking about Nathan but not mentioning him in the setting I was in. It was a huge step.

With such a loss, you feel that every moment you don't talk about your child, you are somehow forgetting him or her and wronging your child in some way. Even though deep down I know this is not the case, the yucky feelings are still there. So it was nice to have interaction about children without feeling this guilt. I have and continue to honor Nathan's memory. I am finding that I also honor him with happy things. Every time I laugh, I feel closer to him.

You see, God wants me to be happy. Laughing and enjoying moments is what God wants me to do. When I do what God wants, I am closer to Him. That same God holds it all in His hands, including our Nathan. Every step forward I take, I am closer to it all.

Chapter 12

Happy Tears

I was up later than usual one evening getting together my art supplies for the cards I periodically send out to grieving parents. I know God will be using these cards for great comfort. I was on my way to bed and felt the urge to check my e-mail.

I was brought to tears. The e-mail was from a woman I had reached out to. I had sent her a card with the link to Nathan's blog, never knowing if it would bless her life, but it planted the seed of healing for God to grow.

She was the first person to request the comfort packet I provide. She wrote and began to tell me her story, and I nearly fell to my knees. God is really in every part of this journey. God told me to write Nathan's blog. God told me to make the comfort packets. God even told me to make the business cards about the blog to leave randomly.

Even though somewhat scared, I knew it would help at least one person. I realized in that moment that God was going to minister to this precious woman exactly the way she needs. God was going to give her the peace we all so desperately need.

That evening, I cried happy tears. I cried in abundance. I cried because that night I saw Nathan's life instead of his death. Through reaching out to grieving parents, Nathan's legacy begins. I realized that his life was not cut short but that his life was short to begin something so much bigger.

When the Holy Spirit speaks to you, it is a moment you will never forget. I will never forget this moment, and I am so grateful for God's presence. This woman blessed me in a way she will never know. It gave me unspeakable joy just to be reminded that God is in control. Every word I write or speak is in God's hands, and He is going to do amazing works.

Nathan,

Mommy misses you to pieces, but tonight, you did not feel so far away. I love you, and don't worry. These are happy tears.

Chapter 13

Our Little Blue Butterfly

—⁓•ᴥᴥᴥᴥ•⁓—

Butterflies in general have many meanings within different cultures, with the most common being symbols for life, love, change or rebirth. Butterflies are also popularly thought to symbolize a person's essence, or soul, either past, present or future.

A blue butterfly is a breathtaking example of Mother Nature at her finest. Because of its beauty, a blue butterfly is often thought to have special meaning and symbolism for those lucky enough to see one. Although seeing a blue butterfly is not a common experience, several species throughout the world are blue—or appear to be—and each holds special significance for its admirers.[8]

—Robin McClure

---

[8]   Robin McClure, "The Meaning of a Blue Butterfly" (Demand Media, Inc., 1999-2013), *eHow.com.*

I thought the introductory quotation was very meaningful because Nathan's memory symbol, if you will, is a blue butterfly. Nathan is my blue butterfly. Amazingly, the article states that it is rare to see them and that a person is lucky to experience a blue butterfly. How true that is. I am lucky to have experienced Nathan's life and am still amazed at the impact his life has on so many people. What a rare butterfly he was indeed. Funny how one little blue butterfly can change your whole life.

I recommend that you find life symbols for your little ones. Find something that speaks to their precious souls, and I promise every time your eye catches these symbols, you will feel nearer to your children.

It never fails that each time I see a blue butterfly in any form, my heart suddenly feels indescribable warmth. Perhaps it is Nathan. Perhaps it is God. Or perhaps it is God holding Nathan. The latter is my personal dream, but the warmth it brings my heart, although indescribable, is divine intervention without a doubt.

Chapter 14

Triggers

We celebrated Nathan's memory when He would have turned seven months old, and it brought a smile to my face, thinking about what he would have been like at that point. The eighth of the month triggers a lot for me. We really try to celebrate the day, talk about him, remember the life of kicks and bounces, and focus on the fact that he was here. The eighth day of the month can triggers tears, but more often, it brings warm feelings and happy memories of our nine months together.

Most days are wonderful. Most days, the things that trigger memories are good thoughts, and the painful ones are bearable. I usually don't pay much attention to what triggers my missing him, but rather I just accept grief when it comes and take a moment to sit with it. But sometimes the triggers are overwhelming as well.

My Pack 'n Play became a trigger that particular week. I saw this Pack 'n Play all day long sitting in my living room. It had became a regular fixture in the living room, and it never bothered me to use it for my nephew or any other visiting children. We currently use several of "Nathan's" things for our little visitors, and they never make me sad. Nathan was never brought home, so he was never in any of them. I don't have a sentimental attachment to these objects. It actually makes me feel good to know that I can use them and not feel sad or guilty. I have put up the items that I do have attachment to in his memory box.

But on this particular night, I was overnight babysitting my nephew. We put the Pack 'n Play at the foot of the bed, and I cried that cry—what I like to call "the weak-knees cry." I realized at that moment that we had not had the Pack 'n Play in that exact position since the night we went to go have Nathan. We had it set up, waiting for our little man, who just simply didn't come home. This was a trigger I wasn't expecting. I see this Pack 'n Play every day, but seeing it at the foot our bed let the floodgates open. I had to just sit on the edge of the bed and have a really good cry.

I also had a trigger when we were moving items into our new church building. All the little ones were going to be there helping. For a split second, my mind deceived me, and I thought, *Where am I going to keep Nathan while I am cleaning so that He will*—The second I thought it, I cried with the realization that Nathan was not here. I know that in my heart all the time, but sometimes it takes my mind a minute. Sometimes this feels like a very bad dream or a very good dream, depending on which parts you focus on. But it feels like a dream all the same.

It is just so strange that he is not here. While my friends are making plans for their little ones, I am not.

But I will say that each of them has helped with this grief. They have all embraced me with so much love that I never feel completely alone without child. I get to love their little ones and be a part of their everyday milestones. It has been such a blessing in a disaster. God knows how my heart will randomly ache, and He provides friends and family members whose little ones are in need of a very special Aunt Sammy.

Triggers are different and hit at the most inconvenient times. I am finding that when grief knocks your knees out, you must simply sit with it for a while. Ignoring your grief is damaging, so I sit with it. I have whatever cry I need. I also allow negativity in these moments. In these moments, I yell all my "why, God … whys?" In these moments, I second-guess my progress. Am I really doing as well as others say I am? I shout all my imperfect curses toward heaven. I even send up the most dreaded question: "Was there something I could have done to make Nathan live?" I let it all fly up, whatever I need to purge, anything that is between the grief I am suffering and the place of peace I need to find. I let it all go up and out, and I wait. I wait for minutes. I wait for days. Sometimes I wait for much longer.

And always, while I am not looking, Peace finally comes back down to me. Deep reassurance is such a gift. It always finds me right where I am. I never have to clean myself up for its arrival. God's grace simply finds me and gives me the peace I need right where I am in His perfect time.

Chapter 15

Greeting Grief

——⚬⚬⚬⚬⚬——

Grief is such an unexpected houseguest. Whether you hate your grief or embrace your grief, it doesn't matter. All that matters is that it has shown up at your doorstep and you have a choice to make: "Do I slam the door in its face and try to ignore it? Could I even run out the back door?" Or, "Do I welcome it in and offer it to stay for coffee? Should we have a short visit that will no doubt be the entire length of my favorite TV show?" At some point, to avoid insanity, you have to make a choice. Do you run from the grief or embrace it?

A few weeks after we lost Nathan, a sweet woman who works at our bank heard our story and opened up about also losing a son many years ago. She told me, "Yes, it is difficult to go forward, but it is possible. It is a choice. You can choose to let the grief overcome you so that you live life as only a shell of who you once were. You can live a life void of God's blessings because your heart is full of regret and anger."

She expressed the flip side as well. "Or you can embrace it and take a journey with it. See what God has for you on the other side of this trial. And gain a peace beyond understanding. You will never move on, but you can move forward."

She, too, is a believer, and I could immediately feel her sweet spirit as she spoke with James and me. She was telling me exactly what I needed to hear at that exact moment. While the world was spinning around us, there was just the three of us. She took valuable time to minister to a couple that needed to see her courage. We needed to be reminded that the power of God can still be found in dark places. Actually, that is where the power of God shines the brightest.

I have carried these words with me though this journey. At the beginning, we all were very afraid of which option I would choose. I had to choose one way to greet my grief. Ignoring it is not an option, and it only leads to insanity. With much prayer and the prayers of my amazing support system, I chose, and now I am able to embrace grief.

I open the door to grief when I feel it knocking. I am finding that if I almost welcome to it, the bad times are less frequent, and the sting is a little less harsh each time. But sometimes grief sneaks in the back door and knocks my knees completely out from under me, expecting me to fall so far I won't even try to get back up.

I sit with it for a minute, giving it some attention. I say, "Good morning, Grief," and then I tell it what we will be doing today. "Grief, we are going to get out of bed, take a shower, enjoy some coffee, talk to the Lord, and see what I need to be doing today, and at some point, I would like to get a nap in."

I am only able to do this because God has given me power through Him. Sometimes grief leaves quickly, and sometimes it lingers. However, it knows that it is not allowed to overcome me.

Even grief must know its place in God's plan. There will be pain. Grief will be part of it, but only within my God's boundaries.

One sleepless night, I was remembering Nathan's features. I could remember his dark hair, button nose, chubby hands, and broad shoulders. But I was very saddened because I could not remember if his eyebrows were light or dark ... or what his feet had looked like. Grief shot me out of bed, and I had to get out Nathan's memory box. I looked through all the photos, frantically trying to find just one picture of his feet. I could not find one.

I was able to see that his eyebrows were lighter than his hair, and I had to accept that some memories just are not going to be so easy to recall. I have to accept that I won't have pictures of every little thing.

I sat with grief for a bit that night. I had a good cry, but it was on my terms.

The fear of forgetting Nathan's features is something I struggle with. I simply have to see him in my mind because memories are all that I have left of him. When you have no tangible evidence of your children, you need your memories to be clear. That is how you see them and bond with them. That is how you respect that they were once living individuals and not just things you held in your dreams.

I am glad that God sets boundaries even on grief almost as if it is there to serve me by keeping me focused. If I stay focused, I have the power to overcome. Grief can sometimes be useful. It can serve as a reminder that we are still in this place, but we are in control of how we chose to meet the circumstances in this place. Pain reminds us that this is not our home.

Chapter 16

Oh Grief, You Trickster

Grief is such a trickster. One night, James and I went to a restaurant we had not been to before. We ran into our favorite server, whom we had not seen since I was very pregnant. She had left another place we had once frequented, and she did not know we had lost Nathan. She was a precious girl, and of course, she greeted us with the most excited words, "How is the baby?"

These moments are dreadful. Most of the time, James and I are concerned with how horrible the other person is going to feel. People feel awful for asking, but it is an honest question. How could they have imagined such a horrible ending to something so wonderful? Of course, we told her and remained strong. We love talking about Nathan, so as painful as the conversation is at first, it always ends up positive and uplifting.

You would think that after these situations happen and because I am able to talk about the incident openly, I am very strong. I am actually not. I am quite weak. I just have a relationship with God and go to Him for strength. Most of the time, I am fine around babies. Most of the time, I see a pregnant woman and smile at the thought. But sometimes it hits me like a wave. Sometimes I simply fall right where I am.

I was in Wal-Mart just a few days after our restaurant encounter and heard a little baby crying at the other end of the store, and I lost it. I had to go into the bathroom and have a good cry. Here I was just a few days before telling my story full of smiles, and the next minute, I am crying in the dog food aisle.

There is just no way to predict when grief's winds will blow your way. Grief is an emotional wind that can suck you up at times. It helps me to give grief its due respect but not give it control. I don't know if that makes sense or not. You have to spend your moments with grief. Never ignore it. It is healthy to cry when needed. It is healthy to be honest when you are not doing so well. But when grief gets out of hand, remind it that this is your journey. God has your journey in His hands, and grief can shake the boat all it wants; however, it is still God's boat.

My boat is not watertight. Sometimes it fills to the tip-top. I just have to keep reminding myself that I am strong enough to tread water, and when I can't anymore, God will pull me out or even drain the water entirely. Or maybe He will do something even more amazing. Either way, I am not alone. I don't have to be strong all the time. I just have to be brave enough to try.

Holding[9]

By Washington Gladded

In the bitter waves of woe,
Beaten and tossed about
By the sullen winds that blow
From the desolate shores of doubt,
Where the anchors that faith has cast
Are dragging in the gale,
I am quietly holding fast
To the things that cannot fail

---

[9] Washington Gladden, "Holding," *Leaves of Gold: An Anthology of Prayers, Memorable Phrases, Inspirational Verse, and Prose* (Brownlow Publishing Co., 1995), 72.

Chapter 17

The Hurt and the Healer

A sad Sunday rolled around. Nathan would have been eight months old this particular Sunday. It was a very difficult day. But the next day, Monday, marked the anniversary of the first time I felt Nathan move. So I choose to replace the sadness with the happiness I felt with every little thump.

Later in the day, I was in the car and had to pull over when I heard this amazing song by Mercy Me called "The Hurt and the Healer."[10] It speaks words that are in my heart. It speaks them louder than I can. Sometimes the power of a song is so great that it leaves me speechless. This song did that for me. All I could do was clutch my chest and cry healing tears. I am not alone.

It speaks of when "Glory meets our suffering," when "the hurt and healer collide." I think it is very powerful that the Creator of all life, values me so much, that he is willing to meet me in my pain. He meets me in my mess and does not scold me for my weakness. He collides with the ugliness and pain of this world and molds it into something worthy of praise.

---

[10] "The Hurt and the Healer," Mercy Me, *The Hurt and the Healer*, 2012.

Lord,

You are my healer. Thank You for Your life and for breathing life back into me today. You never forget me. You knew I needed You before I did. I am humbled by Your love. You are always moving mountains for me, even if You choose to move them one inch at a time.

Chapter 18

A Little Heads-Up

During pregnancy, we all gain a little weight. I did not gain an excessive amount of weight. The problem is that I was big before I got pregnant. I just got rounder and rounder. But I was super cute at the same time. In most cases, after you bring a baby home, you tend to overlook the weight for a while. Because you are so filled with joy, you don't care how big your behind has become. And I am sure the sleepless nights keep you too busy to look at the scale.

But we often forget that when we don't get to bring babies home, our bodies still know we had babies. We have the same post-baby bodies. The same hormonal changes occurred, and it takes some time to get back into shape. For a while, unless you are a superstar with unlimited income for personal trainers and someone to slap carbohydrates away, you may still look a little pregnant. The problem is that grieving mothers are too focused on getting out of bed to even worry about their physical appearances. At about eight months after Nathan's birth, I still looked a little pregnant. Because I was big before Nathan, my belly just seems to stay frozen at about five months pregnant.

This is not really a problem in the grand scheme of things, but I mention it because I was confronted by a kid in the store. I cried about it for hours. I know I cannot be alone in this.

While I was looking at some life vests for my nephew, a kid around eight years old started up a conversation with me. He asked if I was going to the beach, and he told me how much he liked to swim.

Then he asked if I had any little kids. When I told him no, he asked me why I was looking at little kid stuff then. I wanted to tell him that it was none of his beeswax and to shoo him away. Instead, I told him, "I am looking at them for my nephew."

He said, "Oh, that's nice." He walked toward his grandma, gave me a few seconds, came back, pointed at my stomach, and asked, "Are you sure you don't have any little kids?"

I smiled and said, "No, I am sure."

He got bored enough and walked away.

Now I know this was just a kid. But I wish I could say this type of thing has only happened once in the past eight months. It has happened several different ways actually. It has really taught me to never ask a woman when she is due. You just never know the situation. I have been asked several times if I have children. It always stings. Of course, I always tell them about my adopted daughter, Arlene, and smile. But it still stings because I should have two children. I should have a boy and a girl. The American dream, right?

This random kid is not to blame for how I felt. All he did was bring to the surface something I was already struggling with. It is so hard to deal with a post-baby body and not get to enjoy the baby. It is hard to deal with physical changes on top of emotional roller coasters. It is hard to have the motivation to get physically healthy again when I should be toning up by chasing a busy baby boy right now.

I just had to continually remind myself that I live in a fallen world, a world flawed to its core. This makes for painful situations. But the good news is that this pain is only temporary. The pain reminds me that this is not my home. For some reason, Nathan's time with us was limited. For some reason, we are left with a big question mark, and I am left with this flawed body. It simply is what it is. The only thing I can do is hang on and keep standing up and, I guess, get on the dreaded treadmill. Lord, help me!

Chapter 19

Just a Little Reminder

Lord,

I know You guide my steps. I do not do anything without You. I am never without Your affection. But today, Lord, I need reminded. I need reminded that this pain is just a part of the refining fire. I need reminded that one day I will be beyond this and maybe even better because of it. I need You to remind me about who I am to You and that no matter my doubts, I still need to trust You. Today, this very moment, I need You to remind me to believe, even though I cannot see. Remind me that this is just for a little while and that "one day at a time" is an acceptable pace. Remind me that I do not have to move mountains. Remind me that this is Your task and that I only have to climb them. As always, thank You for Your patience. You know my soul well. Sometimes I just need a little reminder. Thank You for Your grace.

Chapter 20

The Eighth day

It was the eighth of the month. I was bummed. I woke up bummed. I showered bummed. I got ready for the day bummed. I did everything bummed the rest of the day. At first, I assumed it was because everything I tried on didn't fit right. Even my shoes seemed tighter. Then I remembered the shoes never really fit right, and that gave me slight relief. Why was I even keeping these silly shoes? I digress.

I spent the day with my sister. We did a little shopping. I used some awesome coupons and even got thirty cents off per gallon of gas. This alone should have brightened my day. I even had a few really good laughs throughout. But still, I was bummed. I even had a slight ache beyond my temples. But I just couldn't name what it was that was bothering me. I mean, besides the obvious, but that is an ache I had become familiar with. I even dare say it was an ache that I was learning to live with. But for some reason, this day was different. I even had pizza for dinner, which usually made me instantly happy on every occasion!

Then I laid my head down and closed my eyes, and quickly, it came to me. This was the eighth of the month—Nathan's nine-month mark. All day, my heart was aching. Even my body was responding. I was out of sorts all day and just couldn't pinpoint why. I am not sure how to feel exactly. Normally, I anticipate the eighth of each month. I anticipate being a little sad and plan accordingly. But this month snuck up on me, and I cried thinking, *I wonder why—Does this make me a bad person? When did I stop counting the days? When did the eighth of the month become just another day? Is this progress or something negative? Is it okay that I did not mark the day?*

The truth is that with or without me intentionally putting this day aside, my heart knew all along. My heart knew what day it was, but it also knew I needed to keep living on this particular day. Maybe it was okay to feel a deeper ache today but to keep going without giving the date itself power. Maybe I shouldn't put the eighth day of each month in a box and stare at it all day long. Maybe my heart will hurt and heal with or without my input. Grief doesn't need my itinerary. God is healing my heart in His time. His time is perfect. Maybe I need to be okay with the fact that I went with the flow today. Truth be told, Nathan is still safe and sound in glory no matter what day it is. I needed reminding that the eighth day of the month could be as special as it could be sad. The eighth day of the month was when James and I finally held him and kissed his chubby cheeks. The eighth day of the month, he was in glory.

The next day, I was shopping, and I saw a wall plaque that I really wanted to buy. The words really spoke to me. I had seen it a few times, and it had always caught my attention. Maybe next week I will go ahead and get it. I just now realized what the words on the plaque truly means. It states, "Keep Calm and Carry On." It's good advice because in the end, the truth is that I hear God best when I am calm and still.

Chapter 21

Mother's Day and Father's Day

—⁓◦◯⦚◦◯⦚◦◯⦚◦◦⁓—

Each year will be a bit painful. That being said, I am still blessed to have peace beyond understanding. Even though our little ones are not with us, we are still mothers. We are still fathers. We can have peace knowing they are safe and sound with the Lord. Fathers, this poem is for you as well because you also share a spiritual chord with your little ones.

The Cord

We are connected
My child and I
By an invisible cord
Not seen by the eye
It's not like the cord that connects us until birth
This cord can't be seen
By any on earth
This cord does its work
Right from the start
It binds us together

Attached to the heart
I know that it is there
Though no one can see
The invisible cord
From my child to me
The strength of this cord
It is hard to describe
It can't be destroyed
It can't be denied
It is stronger than any cord man could create
It withstands the test
Can hold any weight
And though you are gone
Though you're not here with me
The cord is still there
But no one can see
It pulls at my heart
I am bruised
I am sore
But this cord is my lifeline
As never before
I am thankful that God connects us this way
A Parent and child
Death cannot take it away[11]
Thank you to *Lori Beth Blaney*, director of Rachel's Gift, Inc.,
for sending me this poem

---

[11] Poem "The Chord," author unknown.

Chapter 22

A Sobering Question

⸺〰️◦◖⊙✦⊙✦◗◦〰️⸺

Often, the worst times come in the wee hours of the morning. I simply can't sleep, even if I have a prescription that can take down a three-hundred-pound bear. These are the times when I just get out of bed. I have two things I like to do. The first is cleaning. I enjoy a clean house, and after a bit, it helps lull me back to sleep with a sense of accomplishment at the very least.

The second is writing. Journaling puts me more at ease than most things. Even if I start out angry or confused, I end up with the peace that undoubtedly God had planned for me in the first place.

What keeps me up a lot is the very sobering question we and our family get asked a lot: "Are you (they) going to try again?" I will tell you that there is nothing wrong with this question if it's asked at the appropriate time. After Nathan first passed away, this question always took me by surprise. Further down the road, I was better able to answer it, knowing that the person asking was not trying to hurt me at all. I think most people are generally good and mean no harm. I think that they are simply trying to help you place the hope of a new beginning back in your heart. They are simply trying to comfort you in a way that seems appropriate in that moment. They simply want to help you set aside your pain long enough to see the possible hope.

But these are the things that still run through my head when I'm asked such a sobering question: *How could I even answer that question when I still feel like I am in a horrible dream sequence? Also, what do they mean by "try again?" Do they mean try harder not to lose the next baby? Do they mean try not to blame ourselves every moment for losing the last baby? Yes, I want another baby, but not as a replacement! Does even considering it make me a horrible person?* These thoughts and questions swirl around in my head until my eyelids get hot.

Now for those who ask, I know they mean well. I know there is not an ounce of malice in their quandary. It must be difficult for them to know when the appropriate window has been opened for discussion. It must be strange to know when to say just the right words at just the right time.

For those of us who are asked these question, I think it is important to understand that others mean no harm, so simply say what is comfortable for you. Honesty goes a long way, and it has been my experience that others will understand if you say you are unsure how to answer or that it is too painful to discuss right now.

For those who have asked me or will undoubtedly ask in the future, my universal response is this: "We are praying about it." We honestly do, and that is all we can do. We have learned through this tragedy that God really is in control of it all. For us, it is best to pray and be still. Let God's plan work itself out. Satan will attack our grief journey. Scripture proves that we are not alone. Our suffering is only temporary. And that the victor is on the way.

> Be of sober spirit, be on the alert. Your adversary, the devil, prowls around like a roaring lion, seeking someone to devour. But resist him, firm in your faith, knowing that the same experiences of suffering are being accomplished by your brethren who are in the world. After you have suffered for a little while, the God of all grace, who called you to His eternal glory in Christ, will Himself perfect, confirm, strengthen and establish you. To Him be dominion forever and ever. Amen.
>
> —1 Peter 5:8-11

Chapter 23

Oh, Lord

———〰︎◦◦❦◦◦〰︎———

Oh, Lord,

What are You doing with all of this? What am I expected to learn from this pain? Am I doing okay at least for today, anyway? Some days the pain is just so raw, while other days it's painfully far away. I am not sure which feels worse though, and I wonder if I am trusting in You and Your promise to prosper me. Do I even really know what it means to trust You? Will I one day be like Job or Paul? Will I ever be strong and wise and close to You like they learned to be? Will others one day tell my story long after I am gone and tell of my love and devotion to You even through the worst of times? Will I be able to be such a person who can even thank You for this trial? Am I really being refined? I don't feel refined, just burned. Please remind me that one day. I don't even know what, just remind me, Lord. Remind me how important I am to You. Remind me that You are still in control. You know me better than I do. Remind me, Lord. Remind me.

Chapter 24

Walk with Me

There is an illustration from the classic and timeless story of Winnie the Pooh. The illustration depicts Winnie the Pooh and Piglet walking side by side toward the setting sun. The dialogue goes as follows.

> Piglet sidled up to Pooh from behind. "Pooh?" he whispered.
> "Yes, Piglet?"
> "Nothing," said Piglet, taking Pooh's hand.
> "I just wanted to be sure of you."[12]

This illustrates my walk with God some days. I represent the not-so-sure Piglet, and God is the ever-comforting Pooh Bear. Sometimes it makes all the difference just knowing I am not alone. How gracious He is to walk beside me and to remind me He is there ... and for not being offended that I affectionately referred to Him as Pooh Bear.

---

[12] A. A. Milne, *The Complete Tales of Winnie the Pooh* (Dutton Children's Books, 1996).

Chapter 25

Trust in Me Now

Do I trust in God? Do I trust in Him when He is all I have left? Do I trust Him when I can't feel Him? I trust that He is who He says He is. I trust that He is the Great "I Am." I trust that He is my Creator. I want to trust Him completely in every area of my life. But sometime after Nathan died, I started to fear that I only trusted Him in theory. Can this be right? Is it possible that I hold back and choose when I trust God? Do I do this especially when Nathan is involved?

My husband and I visited Nathan's grave on a beautiful evening. We sat for a while, and I just could not hold back the tears. I shook my head at heaven and cried, "Why, God? Why?" Why would God allow me to become pregnant after years of infertility only to take my child away in the end? I wondered, *How do I let Nathan go, and how do I move forward without leaving him behind? What do you want for me? Will Nathan ever know how much we wanted him? Will he ever know how much I ache for him? What do I do next?*

It was one of those waves of grief where I just wanted to pull up a pillow and sleep right there on the cold ground next to

Nathan. It was one of those nights where James had to sweetly pick me up and force to leave. That is always the hardest part—knowing when to leave and knowing when to let go.

This is what I mean by trusting in theory. I do trust that He hears my pleas. I do trust that He has the answers. I do trust that He knows the way. But I often lack faith enough to just let Him lead me without Him telling me what our next move will be. I trust Him to lead, but I struggle with side-seat driving. How can I walk by faith if I feel I need the directions in advance? How can I trust that God knows the way when I desperately want Him to tell me our next move?

Others before me have asked God why. Professor O'Brien at Carson-Newman College wrote the following in a wonderful book that helped me tremendously.

> Jeremiah certainly asked, "Why?" Habakkuk asked, "Why?" So did the Psalmist. Job asked God, "Why?" five times in chapter 3 alone. Even Jesus cried out from the cross, "My God, my God, why have you forsaken me?" … it was precisely because they enjoyed such an intensely intimate relationship with their heavenly Father that each felt the freedom to express His true feelings … Our Lord welcomes honest conversation, which is true prayer. If it were a sin to ask God, "Why?" our Savior would not be sinless.[13]

---

[13] J. Randall O'Brien, PhD, president and professor Carson-Newman College, *Assaulted by Grief: Finding God in the Broken Places* (Mossy Creek Press, 2011), 71

I love this excerpt because I am continually learning to trust God in regards to Nathan—meaning his life, his death, and the life I am left to live. On those days when I shout, "Why?" a thousand times, the excerpt above reminds me that I am not sinning against God by questioning Him. Who else do you talk to about God, except God Himself? Now I do know that the clay should not ask the potter why He made him this way, but for the strugglers out there, what a comfort. How wonderful to at least know that we are not horrible for doing so … and that God, in all His grace, even allows us to question Him.

Trusting God is often a process. You have to have an honest conversation with Him. You have to admit that you are lacking trust. You have to go to God, whom you are not trusting, and ask Him to show you how. It is a full circle of emotion, and it all starts with being honest. Honesty with God is the beginning of it all. I trust that He knows my heart through and through. I admit that I often need a refresher course in trusting God. Honest and open dialogue between Him and me is an ongoing effort on my part. My experience, though, is that my effort never comes back void. His comfort inevitably envelopes me each time, and I can be at peace with Him, even with all my unanswered questions.

> *Lord,*
>
> *Thank You, Lord, for allowing me to try and try again. Thank You for endless chances at the same things. Thank You for speaking to me in the silence. Will You teach me how to trust You properly? I trust You know how difficult I can be. Thank You for the*

whispered discipline. I trust that I need You desperately. I trust You are the only one true God. Can we start there for today? I love You. I trust You knew that before time began.

Chapter 26

Hibernating

———〰⌾❀⌾〰———

I can't help but reference several professors from my sister's former college. They have also lost children, not all of whom were infants. Each told of his or her struggle in a book I found most helpful on my grief journey. It was very encouraging to read.

Late one night, I was all tucked in, and the words jump out at me like the chime of an ice cream truck. Professor Blevins writes, "One of the surprises was my hibernation ... I broke into sobs so easily, I did not want to make others feel ill at ease or embarrass myself ... walking to my car I realized: my fear of seeing others was no greater than other's fear of seeing me!"[14]

This is exactly how I was feeling, but I couldn't find the word to describe my condition. I was hibernating. I was very blessed in that I did not have to go back to work for over a year after Nathan's passing. I busied myself with many other things, but I did not have to force myself back into my old, "normal" routine. Therefore, I had a lot of time in a space I refer to as the

---

[14] Carolyn D. Blevins, MA, associate professor, emerita, school of religion Carson-Newman College, *Assaulted by Grief: Finding God in the Broken Places* (Mossy Creek Press, 2011), 91 and 98.

"in-between." This is a space where I don't really have anything that has my immediate attention. The "in-between" for me felt like I was in this semi-trance state. I was aware of what was going on around me, just not really a part of it. After I read Professor Blevins words, I finally had a word for the "in-between," and hibernating described it perfectly. I became painfully good at keeping myself safe and cozy in my own little cubbyhole. I became so afraid of the interaction that I might face. I feared that I may break down at any moment. Therefore, I avoided social encounters as much as I could. I attended church regularly and even volunteered at my local library, but for the most part, I stayed in a very small circle of people I trusted with my grief. I would constantly worry if people could see the invisible sign on my forehead: "Caution! Grieving mother. May explode at any time!"

I would worry about any reference to Nathan. It could be as simple as this question: "How are you doing?" I would worry because I always seemed to round the corner of the grocery store at the same time as a mommy with her brand-new little boy. I worried that seeing a newborn baby boy would cause me to burst into tears. I would worry by simply anticipating awkwardness and pain. I didn't even think about the fact that the other person was feeling just as apprehensive in not wanting to upset me.

I actually went to a wedding about seven months after Nathan passed and enjoyed myself. But what I kept hidden at the time was that I could not breathe for several seconds as I approached the doors. The air was literally sucked out of my body, and I felt faint. I encountered many loving faces. I had several wonderful embraces. Not once did anyone bring up Nathan, but the fear of it almost kept me at home in hibernation. People were kind. They approached me very gently and found ways to make me laugh. It is troublesome to think that I almost missed the blessing of laughter because of fear.

This is not healthy, but it is not abnormal. I cannot tell you how wonderful it felt to read that someone else felt this way too. How wonderful to know that someone else has struggled with feeling boxed in. If we are not careful, grief can trap us. Loss and grief have a purpose. A purpose I will never understand. God gives no explanation to His ways. Tragedy strikes us all, mostly when we are not looking. But I do not believe this happens for punishment. It is not because of some secret sin in our lives. God allows tragedy for reasons I cannot comprehend. Often, tragedy allows for honest conversation with God. A relationship forms instead of a religion, and we pray intimately, probably for the first time.

Loss and grief do have their place, but it is supposed to be a place where what we have learned cannot hold us. We have to break out of that place and go forward. We have to learn to breathe differently. We have to learn to take different steps because we are not meant to sit still in anguish. We do not always get what we deserve ... or at least what we think we deserve. We get what we get.

We are not in control of what propels us to hibernate. We are only in control of how long we choose to stay in hibernation. I think this offers comfort for a while, but sooner or later, we have to come out of the safe place we have created because it is not realistic. Life is messy and unpredictable, but it is also wonderful and funny. There are moments of joy that we are going to miss if we sit in grief's cocoon too long. Think about this: If a caterpillar stays in the cocoon forever, won't it just die? Eventually, it has to become a new creature, climb out, and fly away.

Chapter 27

Words I Cannot Speak

I have found that music speaks the words I cannot seem to utter. As Nathan's first birthday approached, I had a constant ache in the pit of my stomach. There was a looming cloud of bittersweetness. I thanked God for the miracle that Nathan was, but I still struggled to accept his absence.

In the space of waiting and pain, I have found music to speak louder than ever before. Through music, I was able to praise when I couldn't utter the words in my heart. I will continue to praise God. I will praise because He is worthy and also because through praise, He defeats the Enemy. Praising God will not bring Nathan back, but it does allow me to appreciate where he is. Praise brings me closer to glory, and that is where my son is. I want to be as close to Nathan as I can, and through God, I can do that.

People comment that I am so strong. Actually, I am not. I am very weak. I am heartbroken. I struggle every moment of the day. Sometimes breathing is so difficult that I just want to crumble. But I am okay with being weak. Through my weakness and shaken faith, God is mighty and strong. When you have nothing left and everything you have ever dreamed is lost to you, you find yourself at the end of who you are. You find yourself at the end of all your expectations and plans.

This can be a beautiful thing though, because at the end of who you are, that is where God meets you. He meets you in the broken places when all seems lost. He meets you when you have no direction and every step is shaky. In this place, He gives you unimaginable peace. This peace goes beyond words. In the crying out and times of shouting and the times when my heart screams in agony, there is still peace. I find God in this place of brokenness.

Chapter 28

Angry

The anger stage was very difficult for me to navigate through. I think that was because it often cycled back around. Just when I thought I had said good-bye to anger, here it came again. I was relieved when my last season of anger passed. I was very glad to see it go because it was such a strange, raw emotion.

I see anger as such a strange emotion mostly because it is so often misdirected. When you lose a child, who do you blame? Even when human error or reckless decision is involved, who do you really blame? In the end, doesn't God have the final say? How exactly does a person successfully express anger at the Lord? I think it is human nature to want to blame our Creator when things fall apart. This is all the more reason for me to adore Him. He allows my rants and loves me still.

I think that anger can also be as useful as it is strange. Anger can propel us to another place. Anger can be a handy ladder to scale overwhelming walls. We can actually use anger as a catalyst to propel us higher than we could have before. I think this is why God allows it. Even when anger is directed at Him, He knows it has a purpose in His time. Only in being honest about your anger can you overcome what it was that made you angry in the first place. You have to sometimes meet the beast face-to-face before you can destroy it.

I no longer feel like I am a horrible person for being angry. There is no reason to be ashamed for the angry stages. Mostly, my anger was magnified because everyone else's lives seemed to move right along after Nathan's death. They went to work. They had babies of their own. They laughed and experienced life. My life, however, seemed to stand still. The truth is that others were supposed to move forward. This is the natural progression of life. We are not meant to stay in misery.

In my humanness, I feel week and empty. I am not abnormal for feeling this way. This is what grace is for. God's grace covers the ugliness of my anger and jealousy, and it allows me to be forgiven. It was especially important for me to forgive myself.

Chapter 29

Here and Now

On August 7, 2011, I went to bed and slept. I wasn't sure I would cope with the devastation of the night. But Nathan and I were in a safe place. Somehow, I was blessed with a deep, dreamless sleep.

I was changed. I was different. The life I knew was gone now. I would never be able to go back and breathe life into Nathan. I would have to go forward as a changed person. I would have to breathe life back into myself instead.

There was no closing my eyes and sliding back into the fairy tale of "normal." This was my normal now.

Sara Groves sings a wonderful song titled "Painting Pictures of Egypt: "I've been painting pictures of Egypt, leaving out what it lacked. The future seems so hard, and I want to go back. But the places that used to fit me cannot hold the things I've learned, and those roads closed off to me while my back was turned."[15]

You cannot go back. One minute, your life is this way, and then it is jerked sideways. But still, the sun will rise and set. Still,

---

[15] "Painting Pictures of Egypt," Sara Groves, *Conversations* (3/20/01).

the waves will rise and fall. Still, we must carry on, keeping our eyes open and fixed on the Lord. He will calm the waves.

A year later on Nathan's birthday, August 8, 2012, I learned to look forward and breathe a lot. I learned to rest a lot. In these moments when I am breathing and resting in God, I am also waiting. I am not sure what I am waiting for, but I know God is here with me in the waiting. In the times of silence, it helps to remember that silence is not a punishment. It is a time for us to be still and know. How refreshing to be reminded that it is all right to just be still and not have to figure it all out.

> *Nathan,*
>
> *You are so loved and as near to us now as ever before. On your birthday, we went to the beach. We celebrated your life by laughing and being together as a family. Daddy and I watched the sunset on your birthday. We squished our toes in the sand and thought of you at that very moment. We took deep breaths in and out and breathed you in. We rested in Jesus and breathed whispers all the way to where you are. Happy birthday.*
>
> *We love you,*
> *Mommy and Daddy*

Chapter 30

Shaken

There are times when the pressure behind my eyes is too great a thing. It comes mostly at bedtime. When I close my eyes, it is impossible to not see sad images. The harder I try to push them out, the more they seem to stay. A lot of the times, they include flashes of my hospital stay or Nathan's funeral. I say flashes because the whole scenario seemed like an out-of-body experience at times. Sometimes I only have pieces in my mind. Other things jump out at me, and I remember every horrible detail. I work very hard to control my thoughts and focus on the positive. Most of the time, this is when I journal. I also read book after book. There is a constant flow of the written word in my life. It does help distract my mind.

However, there is this horrible image I just cannot shake. No matter how many late-night prayers, this horrible image of the nurse shaking my belly hits me every night like clockwork. It is a terrible memory and has been very traumatic for me. Why do they do this? I get the idea of it. If you move the belly, the baby will move. But what about the times when the baby does not move? What about the effect this has on the mother? This is what I remember most. I cannot speak for every mother, but I would bet that this keeps a lot of mothers who have had this same experience up at night. It is that moment when you realize what they are checking for. In that moment, you hold your breath, and you are not sure you will ever breathe again.

But alas, you do breathe again. It is a different way of breathing, but it's breath all the same. I think a lot about that moment. That is when I knew in my heart that he was gone before all the monitors and machinery. I guess I knew because a mother just seems to know about her child. He always moved. He moved until he simply didn't.

I struggle with this particular memory the most even to this day. Sometimes I wish I could wipe it from my memory. But I know I really wouldn't. Because to wipe away any part it would take away from the time I had with Nathan. Unfortunately, I must take the painful moments just as I do the wonderful. The painful ones are a part of my story as well, and they are just as important. The painful parts remind me that it was real. Nathan's heart did beat, and the silence of it in the end does not erase the beginning. Sometimes late at night, that is what I focus on—the beginning of Nathan.

I can keep going because Nathan *was* here before I even knew he *was*. He is such an important beginning, and in glory, there is no end. He did not cease to exist, and no amount of shaking can shake that he was "fearfully and wonderfully made." I carried him, and the Lord carried Him the rest of the way.

Chapter 31

The Shack

I am careful in recommending books on grief support. Grief is different for each of us, and what helps me may not help someone else. Whether I am reading fictional or nonfictional accounts, I find that a lot of the phrases I highlight are similar to what I find in my Bible. I feel horrible when I overlook God's Word and hit the bookstores instead. That being said, I do believe God inspires books that truly help people, so I think a healthy balance of both is a wonderful idea.

That being said, I read *The Shack* by Wm. Paul Young. I was admittedly late in the game in reading this book. It seems like everyone has read it. I happened to see a copy on the shelf, and I knew my sister had read it, so I decided to give it a try. I guess the best summary is that it is about a man who loses his young daughter to a violent crime. Later, he receives a letter from "Papa" inviting him back to the shack, where she was killed. He does go, and in turn, he has a personal journey with God that changes him forever.

There is so much in this book that has been reported as controversial. I tend to swim upstream, so controversial doesn't bother me at all. But it may bother you, so take heed. The writer makes God and His Trinity very personalized. I only would recommend it if you are in need of healing your personal relationship with God and you can put religion aside.

Now that that is out of the way, there were two main points that struck my heart with some real power. I struggle with the reason why God doesn't stop our pain, loss, or suffering. You know, the real ugly stuff that hurts to your bones. The reality that God had the power to keep Nathan alive is just one example.

A character from the book named Mack has a similar question. He says, "You may not cause those things, but you certainly don't stop them."

God's character, "Papa," responds, "There are millions of reasons to allow pain and hurt and suffering rather than to eradicate them, but most of those reasons can only be understood with each person's story."[16]

That really struck a chord in me. We will never understand losing Nathan this side of heaven. There were days when searching for those reasons was all I could focus on. It will never make sense, but it can be made good. In Nathan's story, there are moments of pure peace. There are moments of pure sadness. Sometimes there are just pure moments. I think the point is that there are moments at all. There is a story to be told, and every time I tell it, a seed is planted for something, one that only God can grow. God has His reasons, and for me to understand them would take away from the miracle of grace—the grace that I even know God at all. He knows I want to know the reasons, and He knows I am going to

---

[16] Wm. Paul Young, *The Shack* (Windblown Media, 2007), 127.

be angry; however, He loves me anyway, and He is patient and helps me tell Nathan's story despite the fact that I am not getting what I want.

Lastly, Character Mack and I share the want to shed the "great sadness." Mack states,

> The great sadness would not be a part of his identity any longer. He knew that (Missy) wouldn't care if He refused to put it back on. In fact, she wouldn't want Him to huddle in that shroud and would likely grieve for him if he did. He wondered who he would be now that he was letting all that go –to walk into each day without guilt and despair that had sucked the color of life out of everything.[17]

This spoke so loudly to me. After I made it well beyond the year mark of Nathan's passing, I still found myself feeling guilty for not being sad a whole day. If I laugh too loud, do I hurt Nathan's feelings? If I decide not to lie in bed and enjoy the sunshine, am I a horrible mother? If I want to become a new me and leave the coat of sadness behind, what does that say about my love for Nathan? These have been my most painful, innermost struggles in all of this life. How do I move forward without hurting Nathan?

I do not have all the answers, but I do believe that my child is with the Lord in His glorified state. The state of glory is so

---

[17] Wm. Paul Young, *The Shack* (Windblown Media, 2007), 172.

wonderful that it is beyond anything we can imagine. Nathan has experienced the presence of glory. I am not certain if he can see us or not, but if he can see us, I doubt he would want to see us huddled in despair. Nathan is in such a holy presence that sadness does not penetrate. When we pick ourselves up and experience the color of life once again, we do not offend or hurt our loved ones residing in glory. If they could reach down to us and wipe our tears away, we could see their sweet faces in that moment, and we would never feel guilty again.

We would see the safety that holds them every moment, never letting go. We would see peace beyond peace. And I may be alone in saying this, but if I ever saw Nathan that safe and that happy with my own eyes, I would send him back up on a very chubby cloud. I would never want him to be without his perfect completion and the unimaginable peace he will forever experience.

Chapter 32

Brave in Progress

Being brave is something I think I will always work on. For the longest time, I was unable to put grown-up furniture in the room that was to be Nathan's. I must have moved the remaining furniture around a dozen times. I was slowly able to turn a different crib into a toddler's bed for the little ducklings that would come to visit. But I could only handle putting up an air mattress for our adult visitors. For some reason, putting a real bed in what was to be his room seemed very final to me. A big bed made it a guest room and seemed to put the final stamp on it.

Then there was a huge and very painful milestone. I could feel the time had come. It had been building for weeks. So with a heavy heart, we set up our guest bed and made that final gesture. My heart was not ready to do this, but my mind was. My mind said, "Samara, it is time." Maybe it wasn't my mind at all but rather the voice of God. Either way, it was done.

I let it sink in all day. It was a beautiful, breezy, sunshiny day, so I did yard work. I mowed the lawn and cried the entire time. My heart just broke. Later while I was watching TV, one character said to another, "The pain never goes away. You just make room for it." It was a show completely unrelated to my person experience. It was just a line in a script. But it really clung to me.

So after James was all tucked in, of course, I was wide awake. I went in and sat in our "new room." I rocked and rocked and cried and cried. And I stared at that big painful bed. I remembered that quote from TV, and I thought to myself, *It's true … because that is what I did today. I made room for pain.*

It is not going to go away. Nathan is never going to come home and sleep in this room. I had to make room for the pain of growth. I had to start making those final gestures of acceptance. I am going to cry … a lot. It is going to hurt beyond measure. I am going to ask God "Why?" countless times. However, in the end, I must keep doing these things that are hard to do. I must face all the proverbial beds that I simply have to put up. I must be brave and keep trying.

I imagine I will live my whole life and never understand all of this. But I really do believe that one day, I will be in glory and that all of this mystery will be revealed to me. There will not be any more confusion or pain. I believe that if I keep running the race, my eyes fixated on the prize, I will hear, "Well done." Nathan will be there as well, and all of this will not have been for nothing. God has a purpose for it all.

While I wait, I must keep on living. I must remember that my journey will always matter and that those who read these words also matter a great deal. One day, someone will have to face this very same thing, and maybe, just maybe that person will try to be brave too. I am learning that sometimes being *brave* is a process.

Chapter 33

Perspective

I don't have to look too far in life to get perspective. God always puts a certain someone directly in my path just when I need reminding or reflection. After I read the words of a friend of mine in regards to her precious little girl in glory, my heart was changed. Her story echoes what my heart speaks. Her understanding of it all somehow validated my inner chaos.

My father-in-law once told me, "The difference between pain and misery is the lack of growth." It is something I will always remember, and it prompted me to make some very positive steps toward healing. Reflecting back on His words and reading my friend's words made it all come together.

Something about her story planted a seed of healing, and I believe the gap between pain and misery became a bit smaller at that very moment. It wasn't any one thing. Perhaps it was because she has such a sweet spirit despite her loss, and I hope to be like that. I hope to be a beacon for others. I hope that others look at me despite my loss and see my faith in action.

Through this journey, I have struggled with bedtime. Each night, like clockwork, I have fought flashes of my hospital stay.

It hits me as soon as I turn the light off and close my eyes. I can feel each sting like it is still happening. I can see each color that I focused on. It is an extrasensory thing that I pray one day dulls. I pray that one day, I will close my eyes to sleep, and I will just drift off without painful memories. As I read her words, something struck me that I think may help with this and maybe even help my dear readers. She wrote this of her sweet baby girl: "This one precious little soul has brought all of these people together to worship. God was present."

I had forgotten that part. I had forgotten that from the moment we learned Nathan had passed, we were surrounded by believers. It started with our first nurse and ended with the nurse who helped me to the car. There was not one person caring for me who was not a believer. Even my visitors commented on the spirit in the room. God was indeed present, even in our agony. There was so much love and peace in our room despite Nathan's absence. We could all feel it. Even the few nonbelievers in my close circle could feel it. This presence changed us. This presence sustained us, and it still does.

How could I forget this? How could I fail to remember those moments of God's presence instead of the pain? How could I forget those moments when God used Nathan's life for such a purpose as worship? How could I forget how we all cried, and laughed at the same time?

I remember the Scriptures being brought to life and the faith that was in motion. To remember all of this is a blessing. The fact that I have peaceful memories—when I choose to train my brain to search for them—is such a gift. Isn't it just like the Enemy to only remind us of the pain? Isn't it just like him to poke and prod us with the loss? Isn't it just like him to distract us from the glory that was and is still surrounding us? Sometimes I am so focused on trying to breathe that I overlook the fact that God has not forgotten how to breathe for me. Sometimes I am so focused on trying to gain understanding that I forget there is peace beyond it.

Lord, thank You for giving me perspective. Thank You for using my sweet friends and family to get my attention when I ignore You. I am sorry for ceasing to praise You for a moment. Thank You for your sovereignty and for never abandoning me.

Chapter 34

Puzzling Reflection

—⎯ⁿⁿ∽∾⚬∾⚬∾ⁿⁿ⎯—

Now we see things imperfectly, like puzzling
reflections in a mirror, but then we will see
everything with perfect clarity. All that I know
now is partial and incomplete, but then I will
know everything completely, just as God now
knows me completely.

—1 Corinthians 13:12

Even in a place of uncertainty, there can be things you are
certain of. In places of unfamiliar scenery, you can find your way.
You can praise while you are waiting, knowing that something
is just around the corner. Hope does reveal itself. Chasing clarity
before it is time does not allow us to walk by faith.

God is always there. He always has a plan. And even though I
do not understand His ways, I will never cease to believe in Him.
There is light at the end of very dark tunnels, and sometimes I can
see glimpses of it. I can see glimpses of brighter days ahead, and
I must keep my eyes open during the sadness and uncertainty. I

must keep my eyes open because closing them causes me to lose my focus and lands me in the dark again.

The battle is already won for me. I just have to remember that the Lord sees what I cannot. His eyes are always open. In those moments when my eyes are swollen with tears and my knees are weak and all the air seems absent from the room, God sees, stands, and breathes for me. He reminds me that I am not forgotten. I never imagined I could live with such a hurt, and yet here I stand.

Perhaps I am not completely whole, but I am together enough to appreciate these puzzling reflections. Nathan's death is something I will never understand this side of heaven. However, even through the hazy partiality of our story, we are still planting seeds of peace. It all begins, and it all ends with the strength God. He gives it to us. Then we in turn give it to each other. Perhaps we may have even changed someone's perspective at end of this little journey. James and I believe that Nathan's purpose is so much bigger than we will ever understand. He is so important in this life, and he doesn't have to physically be here to leave his mark. One day, all will be revealed to us, and we will be united with our precious boy in complete and perfect glory.

Nathan,

 We love you so much, and we are very proud to tell people that you are part of us forever. We love you and will see you soon.

Until then,
Mommy and Daddy

Lord,

Thank You for working in our waiting. Thank You for building a bridge to You and for allowing Nathan to cross it. Thank You that James and I are also permitted with Your perfect grace to cross this bridge and that we will see our precious Nathan there. We will praise You together. We will see with new sight that is clear and full of the understanding of Your great plan for our temporary pain. Thank You for meeting James and I in our grief with Your perfect grace and for the promise of forever with You and our precious Nathan.

Printed in the United States
By Bookmasters